HEAD SCRATCHERS

TRIVIA

708 Numb-Your-Noggin Questions

that'll Stump Ya!

HEAD SCRATCHERS

TRIVIA

708 Numb-Your-Noggin Questions

that'll Stump Ya!

APPLESAUCE PRESS

LOU HARRY

CONTENTS

CHAPTER

1

★★★★★★★★★

Big Screen/Little Screen

Match the '80s movie teenager to his movie girlfriend.

1) Ferris in *Ferris Bueller's Day Off*   a. Ariel

2) Daniel in *The Karate Kid*   b. Ali

3) Ren in *Footloose*   c. Sloan

4) Blane in *Pretty in Pink*   d. Andie

* *

5) WHAT DOES THE RATING PG STAND FOR?

* * * * * * * * * * * * * * *

6) Put the following Star Trek films in order:

> The Voyage Home, The Wrath of
> Khan, The Search for Spock,
> The Undiscovered Country,
> The Final Frontier

* *

7) In the Jim Carrey movie, how many penguins does Mr. Popper inherit?

NO ONE EVER EXPLAINED TO ME HOW WE'RE SUPPOSED TO SKATE ON ICE WITH WEBBED FEET!

8) Which came first, the movie *The Mighty Ducks* **or the hockey team the Anaheim Ducks?**

* *

9) True or false: There's a movie called *Stop! Or My Mom Will Shoot!*

* * * * * * * * * * * * * * *

10) Complete the titles of these films, which are all part of the National Film Registry.

    a) *The Fall of the House of* _____

    b) *Apocalypse* _____

    c) *The Thing from Another* _____

    d *The Sound of* _____

    e) *Planet of the* _____

    f) *All the King's* _____

    g) *This is Spinal* ____

    h) *In the Heat of the* _____

    i) *Boyz in the* _____

    j) *The* _____ *Stallion*

11) True of false:
There's a movie
called *Santa Claus*
** *Conquers the***
Martians II: The
Elves' Revenge.

● ●

12) How many Superman movies did Christopher Reeve star in?

● ●

13) What was the name of the Superman movie starring Brandon Routh and Kate Bosworth?

14) BESIDES *THE GREEN LANTERN*, WHAT OTHER SUPERHERO FILM WAS RYAN REYNOLDS IN?

  A) *X-MEN ORIGINS: WOLVERINE*
  B) *SKY HIGH*
  C) *THOR*
  D) *X-MEN*

15) True or false: Despite its title, *The NeverEnding Story* did end ... and had a sequel.

16) Jim Carrey played Scrooge in 2009's *A Christmas Carol*. Who played the trio of ghosts?

17) True or false: More people watched the final episode of the TV series *M*A*S*H* in 1983 then watched the Super Bowl that year.

18) Complete the title of each of these Disney Channel original movies.

a) *Sharpay's Fabulous* _____

b) *Lemonade* _____

c) *My Babysitter's a* _____

d) *Camp Rock 2: The Final* _____

e) *Princess Protection* _____

f) *The Cheetah Girls: One* _____

g) *Minute* _____

h) *Wendy Wu: Homecoming* _____

i) *High School* _____

j) *Stuck in the* _____

19) Which came first, *H.R. Pufnstuf* or *Sigmund and the Sea Monsters?*

20) What is the name of the teacher on *The Magic School Bus?*

21) WERE THERE MORE EPISODES MADE OF THE ORIGINAL *BEVERLY HILLS 90210* OR THE ORIGINAL *HAWAII FIVE-O?*

22) Which was not a **TV** show in the 1950s?
    a) *Toast of the Town*
    b) *The Texaco Star Theater*
    c) *You Bet Your Life*
    d) *The Rube Goldberg Show*

23) True or false: **There was once a TV show called *Albonzo Good Morning.***

24) True or false: There was once a TV show called *Holmes and Yo-Yo.*

25) True or false: There was once a TV show called *Tenspeed and Brownshoe*.

26) What does HBO stand for?

27) **What does HGTV stand for?**

28) WHAT DOES DIY NETWORK STAND FOR?

29) Were there more episodes made of *Lassie* or *Cheers?*

30) Match the actor to his show.

a) Jon Cryer	1) *Big Bang Theory*
b) Larry David	2) *Chuck*
c) Billy Gardell	3) *Community*
d) Adrian Grenier	4) *Curb Your Enthusiasm*
e) Zachary Levi	5) *Entourage*
f) Joel McHale	6) *How I Met Your Mother*
g) Nick Offerman	7) *Mike and Molly*
h) Jim Parsons	8) *Modern Family*
i) Jason Segel	9) *Parks and Recreation*
j) Eric Stonestreet	10) *Two and a Half Men*

CHAPTER

2

★ ★ ★ ★ ★ ★ ★ ★

Sports

31) In baseball, who dismissed Giants manager Mel Ott with the phrase, "Nice guys finish last," before replacing him as manager?

* *

32) IN WHAT CITY DID THE TEXAS RANGERS PLAY BEFORE MOVING TO TEXAS?

• •

33) Where did the Baltimore Orioles play before moving to Baltimore?

* *

34) Where did the Oakland A's play immediately before moving to Oakland?

• •

35) What happens if a base runner is hit by a batted ball?

a) Batter is awarded first base
b) Batter is called out
c) Runner is called out
d) Do-over

36) What team was the first—and so far, only—team to lose the first three games of a postseason series, yet come back to win?

    a) Boston Red Sox
    b) Chicago Cubs
    c) New York Mets
    d) New York Yankees

37) What Hall of Famer was nicknamed "The Splendid Splinter"?

    a) Joe DiMaggio
    b) Sandy Koufax
    c) Mickey Mantle
    d) Ted Williams

38) True or false: If the catcher drops strike three, the batter can run to first unless there are less than two outs and a runner on first.

39) In standard scorer's notation, what number represents the shortstop?

40) Match the team to its current home.

a) Citi Field   1) Chicago White Sox
b) Minute Maid Park   2) Houston Astros
c) PNC Park   3) New York Mets
d) U.S. Cellular Field   4) Pittsburgh Pirates

41) True or false: In 1921, Babe Ruth hit 59 home runs by himself, more than any American League team other than his own.

42) WHO DREW THE MOST WALKS IN A SEASON?
- A) WILLIE MCCOVEY
- B) BABE RUTH
- C) BARRY BONDS
- D) TED WILLIAMS

43) True or false: Joe DiMaggio once collected eight hits in a single game.

44) True or false: Since 1900, no team has scored 30 runs in a single game.

45) What is the record for runs scored in one inning?
a) 5   b) 17   c) 25   d) 35

46) Who won the longest MLB game ever played, 26 innings?
a) Braves   b) Cubs
c) Dodgers   d) No one—it was a tie

47) What comedy team immortalized the routine "Who's on First?"

    a) Abbott and Costello
    b) Laurel and Hardy
    c) The Marx Brothers
    d) The Three Stooges

48) TRUE OR FALSE: THERE WAS NO WORLD SERIES FROM 1942-45 BECAUSE OF WORLD WAR II.

Hall of Famer, Yes or No?

49) Maury Wills?

50) Roger Maris?

51) Hack Wilson?

52) Chuck Klein?

53) Mule Haas?

54) Moose Haas?

55) Moose Skowron?

56) Bob Moose?

57) Old Hoss Radbourne?

58) Tim Keefe?

59) WHO LED THE NFL IN RUSHING YARDS EVERY YEAR BUT ONE FROM 1957 TO 1965?

60) The original Cleveland Browns left Cleveland and are now what team?

• •

61) What school won a share of the 1990 National Championship after being saved from defeat when the officials mistakenly awarded the team a fifth down?

a) Alabama   b) Colorado
c) Louisiana State   d) USC

• •

62) What award is given to the top college football player in the nation?

• •

63) What, appropriately, was the

nickname of NFL kicker Lou Groza?

a) The Foot
b) The Leg
c) The Shoe
d) The Toe

64) What team reached four straight Super Bowls, but lost them all?

a) Buffalo Bills   b) Indianapolis Colts

c) Kansas City Chiefs   d) Minnesota Vikings

65) What team has won five Super Bowls and never lost one?

a) Dallas Cowboys   b) Oakland Raiders

c) Pittsburgh Steelers   d) San Francisco 49ers

66) TRUE OR FALSE: BASKETBALL WAS INVENTED BY THE HEAD OF THE P.E. DEPARTMENT AT A SCHOOL IN MASSACHUSETTS WHEN HE WAS ASKED TO CREATE A GAME TO BE PLAYED IN WINTER.

67) True or false: Peach baskets were the first basketball baskets.

68) True or false: Basketball was first played with a tennis ball.

69) True or false: In early women's basketball, players had to stay in assigned areas of the court.

70) True or false: In early women's basketball, there were a limited number of dribbles a player could do.

* *

71) What team did Shaquille O'Neal and Kobe Bryant play for together?

* *

72) Is an official NBA basketball more or less than 30 inches in circumference.

73) HOW MUCH DOES AN NBA BASKETBALL WEIGH?

A) 18 OUNCES   B) 22 OUNCES

C) 26 OUNCES   D) 30 OUNCES

74) True or false: A college basketball player once scored 116 points in a single game.

* *

75) Has anyone ever scored 100 points in an NCAA Division I game?

* *

76) True or false: Bill Russell won 11 NBA Championships.

77) True or false: Until 1913, the bottom of the basketball net was closed.

• •

78) True or false: It was against the rules to slam dunk between 1967 and 1976.

79) In what year was the three-point field goal introduced?
a) 1980 b) 1986 c) 1992 d) 1995

80) TRUE OR FALSE: THE THREE-POINT LINE IS 16.5 FEET FROM THE CENTER OF THE BASKET.

• •

81) In what year was the first NCAA men's basketball championship?
a) 1903   b) 1916   c) 1939   d) 1952

• • • • • • • • • • • ▶

82) True or false: There was an NBA player with the first name Cincinnatus.

CINCINNATUS
A.D. 1967–A.D. 1975

83) Did the United States play in the first soccer World Cup?

84) Who won the first World Cup?

85) True or false: The World Cup was held despite World War II.

86) True or false: The first Women's World Cup was held in 2000.

87) TRUE OR FALSE: THE YOUNGEST PLAYER EVER TO COMPETE IN A WORLD CUP TOURNAMENT WAS 15 YEARS OLD.

88) Did Pele play in the 1958 World Cup finals?

89) True or false: The oldest player ever to compete in a World Cup finals match was 52 years old.

90) True or false: There are three officials in an NHL hockey game—two referees and a linesman.

91) Which of the following was not one of the original six NHL franchises?

a) Boston Bruins

b) New York Islanders

c) Montreal Canadiens

d) Toronto Maple Leafs

92) What team has won the most NHL championships?

a) Boston Bruins

b) Detroit Red Wings

c) Montreal Canadiens

d) Toronto Maple Leafs

93) Is bowling an Olympic sport?

94) WHAT IS A PERFECT SCORE IN BOWLING?

95) Bedposts is a nickname for what in bowling?

96) What split is referred to as the golden gate?

• • • • • • • • • • •

97) How many open frames in a row does it take to have a buzzard?

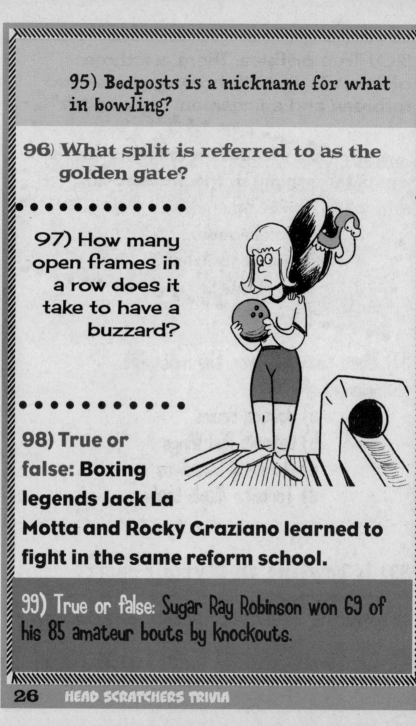

• • • • • • • • • • •

98) True or false: Boxing legends Jack La Motta and Rocky Graziano learned to fight in the same reform school.

99) True or false: Sugar Ray Robinson won 69 of his 85 amateur bouts by knockouts.

100) One of the first closed-circuit television events was a broadcast of the Ken Overlin–Billy Soose middleweight championship fight in 1941. Where did the event take place?

a) Madison Square Garden
b) Carnegie Hall
c) Shea Stadium
d) Atlantic City Convention Hall

● ●

101) TRUE OR FALSE: IDI AMIN, FUTURE LEADER OF UGANDA, WAS A BOXING CHAMPION.

CHAPTER

3

★ ★ ★ ★ ★ ★ ★ ★

Chow Time

102) Which of the following is not a kind of nut?
a) Cobnut   b) Hickory   c) Histon   d) Yeheb

103) WHICH OF THE FOLLOWING IS NOT A KIND OF GRAPE?
A) CABERNET FRANC   B) CATABA

C) PINOT BLANC   D) WALTHAM CROSS

104) Which of the following is not a kind of tomato?
a) Big Boy   b) Moneymaker

c) Sandy   d) Shirley

105) True or false: Most corn grown in the 1800s in the U.S. only produced one large and two small ears.

106) Which of the following is not a kind of corn?
a) Jersey Special   b) Texas Shoe Peg

c) Silver King Wisconsin   d) Reid's Yellow Dent

107) True or false: Mayans used to try to predict the future by reading kernels of corn.

108) Which has more carbs, apples or oranges?

109) Which has more calories, pears or plums?

110) WHICH HAS MORE CALORIES, STRAWBERRIES OR GRAPES?

111) Which has more calories, bananas or apricots?

112) Which has more calories, grapefruit or mango?

113) Woody Allen directed a movie named after what fruit?

114) True or false: Both water and a fruit drinks are traditionally served at a Chinese meal.

115) TRUE OR FALSE: IT IS TRADITIONAL WITH CHINESE FOOD TO LIFT THE PLATE UP TO YOUR FACE AND PUSH THE FOOD INTO YOUR MOUTH WITH CHOPSTICKS.

* * * * * * * * * * * * * * * * *

116) What is a fried burrito called?
   a) Quesadilla   b) Chimichanga
   c) Tostada   d) Bunuelos

* *

117) What company makes Pop-Tarts?

118) Pop-Tarts were once advertised with a toaster character named...
   a) Marvin   b) Milton
   c) Muggsy   d) Manny

119) What cereal was advertised with the line "It's just like eating up the alphabet"?

120) What popular breakfast cereal was originally called Apple O's?

121) Bart's Peanut Butter Chocolate Crunch was a spin-off of what TV show?

122) WHICH OF THE FOLLOWING IS NOT A DISCONTINUED MCDONALD'S FOOD ITEM.
- A) MCDLT
- B) ARCH DELUXE
- C) HAMBURGLER SUPREME
- D) ONION NUGGETS

****

123) True or false: The Burger King fish sandwich used to be called the Big Swimmer?

****

124) Burger King was first known as Insta-Burger King.

125) Which burger chain had the first deal with Lucasfilm to sell Star Wars glasses?

126) The first McDonald's restaurant opened in ...
- a) 1933
- b) 1940
- c) 1949
- d) 1954

127) True or false: The original McDonald's mascot was a chef named Speedee.

* *

128) Did McDonald's open first in Japan, France, or El Salvador?

* *

129) TRUE OR FALSE: MCDONALD'S WON A LAWSUIT THAT HAS KEPT THE DEROGATORY TERM MCJOB OUT OF MERRIAM-WEBSTER'S COLLEGIATE DICTIONARY.

* *

130) True or false: A copycat restaurant called MaDonalds opened in Kurdistan and sold Big Macks.

* * * * * * * * * * * * *

131) Which has more locations, Subway or McDonald's?

* *

132) True or false: Domino's Pizza was originally called DomiNick's.

133) In what book does the character Long John Silver appear?

● ● ● ● ● ● ● ● ● ● ● ● ● ● ● ● ● ● ● ●

134) True or false: McDonald's Corp. owns Dominos Pizza.

135) True or false: Coca-Cola owns Burger King.

136) ACCORDING TO ITS ADS, IT TAKES TWO HANDS TO HANDLE WHAT SIGNATURE BURGER?
  A) BIG JACK   B) WENDY'S TRIPLE
  C) BIG MAC   D) WHOPPER

● ●

137) What building was White Castle restaurants' architecture adapted from?
  a) The Empire State Building
  b) Westminster Abbey
  c) Elsinore
  d) Chicago Water Tower

● ●

138) Arthur Treacher's Fish and Chips was named after:
  a) A British prime minister
  b) An actor
  c) A cricket player
  d) A naval officer

139) On what holiday does Nathan's Famous hold its annual hot dog eating contest?

● ●

140) How many hot dogs did the 2011 winner eat?

● ● ● ● ● ● ● ● ● ● ● ● ● ● ● ● ● ● ● ●

141) How much time do contestants in the Nathan's Famous hot dog eating contest have to eat as many hot dogs as they can?

● ●

142) Do they have to eat the buns?

● ●

143) DO WOMEN COMPETE SEPARATELY OR WITH MEN IN THE NATHAN'S FAMOUS HOT DOG EATING CONTEST?

● ●

144) Where is the Nathan's Famous hot dog eating contest held?

145) What city is considered the biggest consumer of Slurpees?

a) Winnipeg, Canada
b) Chicago, Illinois
c) Atlanta, Georgia
d) Jackson, Mississippi

146) True or false: The P.F. in the restaurant name of P.F. Chang's refers to an ancient Chinese dynasty.

147) True or false: The first Cheesecake Factory was in Beverly Hills, California.

148) True or false: Howard Johnson's was once the largest sit-down restaurants chain in America.

149) How many flavors of ice cream did Howard Johnson's boast of having during its early days:
a) 12   b)   18   c) 28   d) 36

150) WHICH CAME FIRST IN THE EVOLUTION OF PIZZA, THE CHEESE OR THE TOMATO SAUCE?

151) Pizza as we know it is largely believed to have been conceived in...
a) Naples   b) Verona
c) Rome   d) Cleveland

152) True or false: **Margherita pizza is named for Queen Margherita of Savoy.**

153) True or false: Pepperoni is the most requested topping on pizza.

154) **What month is National Pizza Month?**

155) True or false: The name ketchup comes from Ke-chiap, a Chinese fish sauce.

156) True or false: Snickers contains almonds.

157) WHAT YELLOW-WRAPPED, CHOCOLATE-COVERED PEANUT BAR WAS HERSHEY'S SECOND PRODUCT, AFTER THE HERSHEY BAR?

158) According to Mr. Owl, how many licks does it take to get to the center of a Tootsie Pop?

159) What color of M&Ms was scrapped in 1975, and then reintroduced in 1987?

160) What do you get if you combine chocolate, marshmallows and graham crackers?

161) True or false: both chocolate and vanilla come from beans.

162) True or false: A food can be called "sugar free" and still have some sugar in it.

163) True or false: **Ice cream was originally called iced cream.**

★ ★ ★ ★ ★ ★ ★ ★ ★ ★ ★ ★ ★ ★ ★ ★ ★ ★

164) WHAT MINERAL CONTROLS AND LOWERS THE TEMPERATURE OF INGREDIENTS DURING THE MAKING OF ICE CREAM?

165) What was introduced at the 1904 World's Fair in St. Louis?
    a) The first ice cream sundae
    b) Sprinkles/jimmies
    c) Neapolitan ice cream
    d) The edible cone

166) Soft ice cream involves increasing the amount of what?

★ ★ ★ ★ ★ ★ ★ ★ ★ ★ ★ ★ ★ ★ ★ ★ ★ ★

167) True or false: **George Washington served ice cream to guests.**

168) True or false: Sprite used to describe its flavor as "lymon."

169) Which came first, Sprite or 7-Up?

★ ★ ★ ★ ★ ★ ★ ★ ★ ★ ★ ★ ★ ★ ★ ★

170) TRUE OF FALSE: 7-UP HAS HAD THE SAME FORMULA SINCE THE 1940S.

CHAPTER

4

Games

171) On early Egyptian playing cards, which was not a symbol.
a) Cups
b) Coins
c) Swords
d) Crowns

172) Which country added the joker to the playing card deck?

173) On a Battleship game board, what is the highest letter?

174) True or false: Battleship was originally a pencil-and-paper game called Broadsides: The Game of Naval Strategy.

175) Does a game of Othello start with four pieces in the center of the board or at the corners?

176) In Othello, who makes the first move, light or dark?

177) IN OTHELLO, CAN PIECES PLACED IN THE CORNERS BE FLIPPED?

178) When did the Pokémon Trading Card Game first enter the Japanese market?
a) 1976   b) 1986   c) 1996   d) 2001

179) Which is not the color of an Uno card?
a) **Red**   b) **Orange**   c) **Green**   d) **Blue**

180) True of false: There is one Draw Three card in a standard Uno game.

181) True or false: Uno was created by the same people who developed the Pizzeria Uno restaurant chain.

182) True or false: Yahtzee has been played on *Family Guy* and *South Park*.

* * * * * * * * * * * * * * * * * *

183) How many different dice sizes are there in Challenge Yahtzee?

* *

184) WHICH IS A BOARD GAME, SHOWDOWN YAHTZEE OR TRIPLE YAHTZEE?

* *

185) True or false: Yahtzee is based on a similar game called Yacht.

* *

186) **True or false: In backgammon, if you have six consecutive points with at least two checkers of your color on each it's called a bammo.**

187) True or false: In backgammon, if your role lands on a checker, both dice are to be rerolled.

188) Can a backgammon player pass his or her turn?

189) Which of the following is not a Cranium category?
a) Word Worm
b) Fact Junkie
c) Creative Cat
d) Star Performer

190) How much time does it take a Pictionary timer to run out?

191) TRUE OR FALSE: CHEESE PIECES WERE ADDED TO MOUSE TRAP IN THE 1970S.

* *

192) When was Dungeons and Dragons first published?
a) 1968
b) 1974
c) 1979
d) 1987

193) Who co-created
Dungeons and Dragons?
   a) Gary Gygax
   b) Gary Varval
   c) Gary Gilmore
   d) Gary Coleman

• •

194) What company now publishes
Dungeons and Dragons?
   a) Wizards of Westfield
   b) Wizards of the Coast
   c) Wizards and Warriors
   d) Wizards of Warrior Place

195) Who leads a game of Dungeons
and Dragons?
   a) The oldest player
   b) The Dungeon Master
   c) The Cerberus
   d) The Leading Troll

196) How many extra points do you get for using
all seven of your letters in one play in Scrabble?

197) True or false: Scrabble tiles are made from the wood from elm trees.

198) TRUE OR FALSE: SCRABBLE WAS ORIGINALLY PLAYED WITHOUT A BOARD.

199) How many points is an **M** worth in a game of Scrabble?

200) Which of the following words is impossible to get in Scrabble without using a blank?

  a) Quagmire   b) Quizzical   c) Zipper   d) Albatross

201) In Risk, what continent has the most territories?

202) Which of the following is not a territory in Risk?

        a) Yakutsk   b) Ukraine
        c) Ural   d) Uganda

203) How many continents on the Risk board?

204) What is the largest denomination of cash in the Game of Life?

205) WHICH OF THE FOLLOWING WAS NOT FEATURED IN A SPECIAL EDITION OF THE GAME OF LIFE?

- A) MONSTERS, INC.
- B) INDIANA JONES
- C) THE WIZARD OF OZ
- D) THE CHRONICLES OF NARNIA

206) What was the extra murder weapon in the 50th anniversary edition of Clue?
a) A bottle of poison   b) A hand grenade
c) A blackjack   d) A submachine gun

207) How much do you get for passing Go in Monopoly Here and Now?

208) True or false: The World Monopoly Tournament has aired on ESPN.

209) True or false: Atlantic City has never hosted the World Monopoly Tournament.

● ●

210) What kind of hat is a Monopoly playing piece?

● ●

211) How many utilities are in a Monopoly game?

● ●

212) HOW MANY HOTELS IN A MONOPOLY GAME?

● ●

213) How many monopolies consist of just two properties?

214) True or false: The real B&O Railroad did not serve Atlantic City.

215) How much do you get for passing Go in regular Monopoly?

● ●

216) True or false: Parker Brothers does not allow slot machines to use Monopoly logos and characters.

217) What is the only property you can land on by drawing the "Go Back 3 Spaces" card?

****

218) True or false: If all the houses or hotels in the box have been purchased, you can use pennies for houses and nickels for hotels (or whatever markers you have available).

****

219) How much money does each player start with in Monopoly?

220) IF YOU ROLL NOTHING BUT SEVENS THE ENTIRE GAME, WHAT IS THE ONLY PROPERTY YOU WILL NEVER LAND ON?

• •

221) True or false: **in British Monopoly, the Income Tax space is called "Super Tax."**

222) Which space on the board is landed on the most?
a) Go   b) Jail
c) Illinois Avenue   d) Boardwalk

223) Which property completes the monopoly if you own North Carolina and Pennsylvania Avenues?

224) Which property completes the monopoly if you own Illinois and Indiana Avenues?

* *

225) Which property completes the monopoly if you own New York and Tennessee Avenues?

* *

226) How much money is in a Monopoly game box?
   a) $10,540
   b) $14,500
   c) $20,580
   d) $26,665

227) In a crossword puzzle, which clues are usually listed first, the across clues or the down clues?

228) TRUE OR FALSE: A CROSSWORD CREATOR IS A CRUCIVERBALIST.

229) What does an abbreviation in a clue indicate?

230) Does the server in Four Square serve from the highest-ranking square to the second highest ranking square or to the lowest ranking square.

231) In Four Square, do your feet have to stay in your square?

232) In hopscotch, does a marker that lands on a line count?

233) How many points is a ringer in horseshoes?

234) How many points is a close shoe in horseshoes?

235) IS IT GENERALLY BETTER TO GO FIRST OR LAST IN CROQUET?

236) Do you have to go through wickets in order in croquet?

• •

237) In croquet, the person whose turn it is is called the _____
   a) Striker
   b) Hitter
   c) Pounder
   d) Batter

238) How close does a horseshoe have to be to the stake to be a close shoe?

239) How many points is a leaner in horseshoes?

• •

240) What's another name for a close shoe in horseshoes?
   a) A neary
   b) An incher
   c) A shoe in count
   d) An almost

CHAPTER

5

★ ★ ★ ★ ★ ★ ★ ★ ★

Animals

241) True or false: The duckbill platypus has poison-tipped spurs behind each leg.

MATCH THE ANIMAL TO THE NAME FOR ITS HABITAT:

242) PENGUIN

243) BEAVER

244) WOLF

245) HARE

A) LODGE

B) DOWN

C) LAIR

D) ROOKERY

Match the animal to its young:

246) Elephant

247) Fox

248) Horse

249) Goat

a) Kid

b) Foal

c) Cub

d) Calf

250) True or false: There are more than 10,000 species of mammals in the world.

****

251) Are mammals warm-blooded or cold-blooded?

Match the scientific name to the species that it includes.

252) Edentata   a) **Kangaroo**

253) Carnivora   b) **Rat**

254) Proboscidea   c) **Man**

255) Marsupialia   d) **Elephant**

256) Rodentia   e) **Dog**

257) Primates   f) **Armadillo**

258) True or false:
All aardvarks
weigh less than
100 pounds.

TIME TO DIET!

259) Does an aardvark have more claws on its front feet or its back feet?

260) CAN AN AARDVARK MOVE ITS EARS INDEPENDENTLY OF EACH OTHER?

261) True or false: **An African buffalo's horns can help it float in water.**

262) True of false: An African buffalo keeps all of its hair until it dies.

263) True or false: The African wild dog runs on its toes.

264) True or false: The African wild dog always has a black-tipped tail.

265) True or false: Each African wild dog has a different pattern in its coat.

266) How many toes are there on each paw of an African wild dog?

• • • • • • • • • • • • • • • • • • • •

267) WHICH USUALLY HAS A SHORTER TAIL, THE AMERICAN BISON OR THE EUROPEAN BISON?

• • • • • • • • • • •

268) True or false: The shape of an American bison's face can help you figure out its age.

• • • • • • • • • • •

269) True or false: The fennec is the smallest of all foxes.

• • • • • • • • • • • • • •

270) True or false: The Arctic fox has fur on both the top and bottom of its paws.

• •

271) True or false: The Arctic fox can sleep on ice.

272) True or false: The Arctic fox has pointed ears.

273) True or false: An armadillo's front legs are about twice as long as its back legs.

YOU'D LOOK MORE FIERCE IF YOUR SHIRT DIDN'T HAVE A PIZZA STAIN ON IT!

MESS WITH ME!

274) WHICH ARE LONGER, A BADGER'S FORE CLAWS OR ITS HIND CLAWS?

275) True or false: A badger cannot run.

276) Which tends to be smaller, a black bear or a polar bear?

277) How many toes does a black bear have on each paw?

278) True or false: A black bear's teeth are completely grown by its first birthday.

● ● ● ● ● ● ● ● ● ●

279) Which tends to have a shorter coat, the black bear or the grizzly bear?

● ●

280) Which can grow taller, a grizzly bear or a Kodiak bear?

● ●

281) TRUE OR FALSE: BECAUSE OF ITS RELATIVELY SMALL EARS, GRIZZLY BEARS CANNOT HEAR VERY WELL.

282) True or false: Grizzly bears have no lips.

283) True or false: The hands of a koala each have two thumbs.

* * * * * * * * * * * * * * * * *

284) Koalas and wallabies are *diprotodonts,* which means...
    a) Their feet and hands are different shapes
    b) They have shorter front limbs than back limbs
    c) They are marsupials with two incisor teeth in their lower jaw
    d) They eat eucalyptus

285) True or false: Polar bears eat mostly meat.

286) Is a polar bear's skin white?

287) When running, do a hare's hind legs ever go in front of its forelegs?

288) Which has a longer hind leg, a hare or a rabbit?

* * * * * * * * * * * * * * *

289) TRUE OR FALSE: THE TERM "HAIRLIP" COMES FROM THE SHAPE OF A HARE'S LIP.

290) True or false: Young camels have more incisor teeth than adult camels.

291) True or false: If a camel is starving, its hump may slide to one side.

* * * * * * * * * * * * * * *

292) True or false: A camel has no eyelashes.

* * * * * * * * * * * * * *

293) True or false: A beaver's tale can store fat.

294) Which is usually taller, a leopard or a cheetah?

295) What color are the backs of a cheetah's ears?

296) TRUE OR FALSE: A CHEETAH CAN RETRACT ITS CLAWS ALL THE WAY INTO ITS PAWS.

297) True or false: Leopards have hair on their tongues.

298) Is a snow leopard bigger or smaller than a regular leopard?

299) About how many muscle units are in an elephant's trunk?
- a) 1,000
- b) 10,000
- c) 100,000
- d) 1,000,000

300) Which has a spine that curves upward, an African or an Asian elephant?

301) True or false: Elephants cannot run faster than 20 mph.

302) The tongue of an adult giant anteater is about:
a) 9 inches long
b) 24 inches long
c) 48 inches long
d) 64 inches long

303) TRUE OR FALSE: THE ANTEATER'S NOSTRILS ARE NEAR ITS EYES.

304) True or false: The anteater walks on its claws.

• • • • • • • • • • • • • • • • • • • •

305) True or false: **All of an anteater's claws are the same size.**

• • • • • • • • • • • • • • • • • • • •

306) Which are heavier, male anteaters or female anteaters?

• • • • • • • • • •

307) Can the giant panda see well at night?

• • • • • • • • • • •

308) The giant panda's "false thumb" is actually...
   a) A chunk of fatty tissue
   b) A large wrist bone
   c) Excess skin
   d) A claw

309) How many vertebrae in a giraffe's neck?
  - a) 7
  - b) 70
  - c) 700
  - d) 7,000

● ●

310) TRUE OR FALSE: A GIRAFFE'S FRONT LEGS ARE ALMOST TWICE AS LONG AS ITS HIND LEGS.

● ●

311) What color is a giraffe's tongue?
  - a) Red
  - b) Black
  - c) Pink
  - d) Tan

● ●

312) What color are a giraffe's eyes?
  - a) Green
  - b) Blue
  - c) Brown
  - d) Black

CHAPTER

6

Comics

313) Which came first, Detective Comics or Action Comics?

★ ★ ★ ★ ★ ★ ★ ★ ★ ★ ★ ★ ★ ★ ★ ★

314) WHO CAME FIRST, SUPERMAN OR MANDRAKE THE MAGICIAN?

★ ★ ★ ★ ★ ★ ★ ★ ★ ★ ★ ★ ★ ★ ★ ★

315) True or false: In 1946, comic books outsold traditional books.

316) True or false: **There were comic-book burnings in Chicago and New York in the 1960s by people who thought they were harmful to young people.**

317) When did the U.S. Postal Service honor comic books with a series of Superhero stamps?

a) 1955   b) 1966

c) 1987   d) 2006

318) True or false: The 2006 U.S. Postal Service Superhero stamps did not include Batman.

319) When was the Comic Code Authority created?
a) 1954   b) 1960   c) 1964   d) 1971

★ ★ ★ ★ ★ ★ ★ ★ ★ ★ ★ ★ ★ ★ ★ ★

320) True or false: Mad magazine was first published as a comic book.

★ ★ ★ ★ ★ ★ ★ ★ ★ ★ ★ ★ ★ ★ ★ ★

321) TRUE OR FALSE: DC IS SHORT FOR *DETECTIVE COMICS.*

★ ★ ★ ★ ★ ★ ★ ★ ★ ★ ★ ★ ★ ★ ★ ★

322) What Art Spiegelman two-volume illustrated comic-book memoir earned critical and mainstream acclaim in 1986?
a) *Morris*   b) *Maus*
c) *Mr. Mouse* d) *Mess*

★ ★ ★ ★ ★ ★ ★ ★ ★ ★ ★ ★ ★ ★ ★ ★

323) Time magazine's list of the 100 best English language novels from 1923 to 2005 included which comic book?

324) True or false: A comic book was nominated for the 2006 National Book Awards.

325) Which of the following films was not based on a comic book/graphic novel?

a) *Road to Perdition*   b) *Ghost World*

c) *Pulp Fiction*   d) *A History of Violence*

* * * * * * * * * * *

326) True or false: About 50 comic books are added to the Library of Congress's collection every month.

* * * * * * * * * * *

327) True or false: Popular British comic books have included *The Beano*, *The Dandy*, and *Viz*.

328) In 1947, *Classic Comics* became known as what?

    a) *Classics Comics*
    b) *Classics Illustrated*
    c) *Illustrated Classics*
    d) *Comic Book Classics*

329) True or false: According to the 1954 Comics Code, good always had to triumph over evil.

* * * * * * * * * * * * * * * * * * * *

330) According to the Comics Code, all but the following were never allowed to be presented disrespectfully:
a) **Judges**   b) **Policemen**
c) **Teachers**   d) **Government officials**

DC OR MARVEL?

331) Spiderman

332) Wonder Woman

333) Super-Man

334) The Hulk

335) Batman

336) Fantastic Four

337) True or false: The Flash, Hawkman, and the Green Lantern were all introduced in the same year.

• •

338) Which came first, Spider-Man or the Human Torch?

• •

339) The Fantastic Four first appeared in...
a) 1941   b) 1961   c) 1971   d) 1981

340) WHAT SUPERPOWER DOES MR. FANTASTIC HAVE?

341) What superpower does Sue Richards have?

• •

342) What is the superhero name for Johnny Storm?

343) What is the superhero name for Ben Grimm?

• • • • • • • • • • • • • • • • • • • •

344) Match the villain to his or her nemesis.

a) Black Manta	1) Blade
b) Bullseye	2) Thor
c) Cheetah	3) Teen Titans
d) Deacon Frost	4) Batman
e) Deathstroke	5) The Punisher
f) Dormammu	6) Judge Dredd
g) Eivol Ekdol	7) Daredevil
h) Jigsaw	8) Aquaman
i) Judge Death	9) Wonder Woman
j) Loki	10) Dr. Strange

• • • • • • • • • • • • • • • • • • • •

345) In what language did *The Adventures of Tintin* first appear?

a) English   **b) Japanese**

c) French   **d) Italian**

346) The Adventures of Tintin was created by artist Georges Remi whose pen name was...

a) Hergé   b) Hugo   c) Huggy   d) Higgy

347) WHAT IS TINTIN'S DOG'S NAME?

A) SNOWY B) SONNY C) ZIGGY D) SLAPPY

348) Tintin is a...

a) Hunter   b) Reporter
c) Police officer   d) Teacher

349) Archie Andrews first appeared in...

a) Pep Comics   b) Pop Comics
c) Plop Comics   d) Ploop Comics

350) Who is Archie's best friend?

351) Which one has black hair, Betty or Veronica?

352) True or false: Archie Comics sued the band the Veronicas for infringing on its trademark.

353) What is Archie's hometown?

354) WHAT INSTRUMENT DOES JUGHEAD PLAY?

355) True or false: **Jughead has a younger sister named Chrysanthemum.**

356) The comic Brenda Star was first published in 1940. What was her job?

    a) **Firefighter**   b) **Superhero**
    c) **Reporter**   d) **Pilot**

357) True or false: One of the first comic strips was called *Little Nemo in Slumberland.*

358) True or false: Tom Wilson worked at a greeting card company when he created Ziggy.

359) What was the first comic strip to win a Pulitzer Prize for Editorial Cartooning?

    a) *Pogo*   b) *Doonesbury*
    c) *Hi and Lois*   d) *The Far Side*

360) According to the comic character Cathy, the four basic guilt groups are Food, Love, Mother, and...

  a) Home　　　b) Career

  c) Movies　　d) More Food

* *

361) WHAT IS GARFIELD'S OWNER'S NAME?

* *

362) What is Garfield's owner's dog's name?

* *

363) Where does Garfield artist Jim Davis live?

  a) Ohio　　　　　　b) New York

  c) Pennsylvania　　d) Indiana

* * * * * * * * * * * * * * * * * * *

364) True or false: Jim Davis is still the only illustrator of Garfield comics.

* * * * * * * * * * * * * * * * * * * *

365) In Peanuts, who is older, Charlie Brown or Sally Brown?

* * * * * * * * * * * * * * * * * * *

366) What is Lucy's last name?

* *

367) What is Linus's younger brother's name?

368) WHAT DOES PEPPERMINT PATTY
CALL CHARLIE BROWN?

* * * * * * * * * * * * * * * *

369) What color is Schroeder's hair?

* * * * * * * * * * * * * * * *

370) What position does Schroeder play
on Charlie Brown's baseball team?

* *

371) True or false: Charlie
Brown's father is a chef.

* * * * * * * * * * * * * * * *

372) Is Charlie Brown's pen pal a boy or a girl?

* * * * * * * * * * * * * * * * *

373) True or false: Snoopy has a brother
named Henry.

* * * * * * * * * * * * * * *

374) Who is Snoopy's enemy when he
is fantasizing about being the World
War I Flying Ace?

* *

375) WHAT DOES SNOOPY CALL HIS DOGHOUSE
WHEN HE IS HAVING A WORLD WAR I FANTASY?

CHAPTER

7

★★★★★★★★★

376) Stefani Germanotta is better known as whom?

377) IS ISSUR DANIELOVITCH DEMSKY BETTER KNOWN AS KIRK DOUGLAS OR MICHAEL DOUGLAS?

378) True or false: Actor Stewart Granger was born under the name James Stewart, but had to change it because it was already taken.

****

379) True or false: Actor Michael Keaton was born under the name Michael Douglas, but had to change it because it was already taken by another actor?

380) What actress, born Dianne Hall, was the mother in the *Father of the Bride* movies?

381) Alexandra Molinsky is better known as what comedian?

382) True or false: Betty Jo Perske is better known as Betty White?

Match the initials to the name.
383) L.A.   a) Clothier Bean
384) L.B.   b) Defensive end Greenwood
385) L.C.   c) Movie producer Mayer
386) L.L.   d) Record producer Reid

387) TRUE OR FALSE: J.K. ROWLING'S GIVEN NAMES ARE JOANNE KATHLEEN.

388) William Henry McCarty Jr. is better known as what western outlaw?

389) Samuel Clemens is better known as whom?

390) David Cameron: British prime minister or Google executive?

391) John Lasseter: Arizona congressman or head of Pixar?

392) David Petraeus: CIA director or building designer?

393) GERRY ADAMS: FORMER SPICE GIRL OR IRISH RESISTANCE LEADER?

394) Isabel Allende: Chilean writer or world-renowned chef?

395) Dave Barry: **Humor writer or founder of Amazon.com?**

396) Christopher Buckley: Magazine editor or Republican presidential candidate?

397) Mark Burnett: *Survivor* **producer or syndicated radio host?**

398) Van Cliburn: Pianist or silent movie actor?

399) Stephen Ambrose: Historian or jockey?

400) JOAN BAEZ: FIRST LADY OF SPAIN OR FOLK SINGER.

• •

401) Elizabeth Blackwell: First woman to fly in space or first woman to graduate from medical school.

• • • • • • • • • • • • •

402) Dian Fossey: Gorilla researcher or fashion designer?

• • • • • • • • • • • • • • • • • • • •

403) Are composers Johann Sebastian Bach and P.D.Q. Bach related?

• • • • • • • • • • • • • • • •

404) Are quarterback Tom Brady and former Treasury Secretary Nicholas Brady related?

405) Are former baseball commissioner A. Bartlett Giamatti and actor Paul Giamatti related?

● ●

406) Are comedienne Carol Burnett and *Survivor* creator Mark Burnett related?

● ●

407) ARE BROADWAY COMPOSERS RICHARD AND MARY RODGERS RELATED?

● ●

408) Are authors Henry and William James related?

● ●

409) Are author Charles Dickens and country star Little Jimmy Dickens related?

● ●

410) Are *Moby Dick* author Herman Melville and alt-rock musician Moby related?

411) Are actors Tom and Colin Hanks related?

412) Are former TV newswoman Maria Shriver and former vice-presidential nominee Sargent Shriver related?

413) Are billionaire John D. Rockefeller and Vice President Nelson Rockefeller related?

414) ARE PRESIDENT RONALD REAGAN AND TALK-SHOW HOST MICHAEL REAGAN RELATED?

415) Are billionaire J. Paul Getty and actress Estelle Getty related?

416) Are comedian David Spade and designer Kate Spade related?

417) Are actress Olympia Dukakis and former presidential candidate Michael Dukakis related?

418) What baseball player is nicknamed A-Rod?

★ ★ ★ ★ ★ ★ ★ ★ ★ ★ ★ ★ ★ ★ ★ ★

419) What baseball player was nicknamed K-Rod?

420) What NBA player was nicknamed T-Mac?

421) WHAT MUSICIAN IS NICKNAMED T-BONE?

★ ★ ★ ★ ★ ★ ★ ★ ★ ★ ★ ★ ★ ★ ★ ★

422) What NBA player was nicknamed K-Mart?

★ ★ ★ ★ ★ ★ ★ ★ ★ ★ ★ ★ ★ ★ ★ ★

423) St. Louis Cardinals reliever Marc Rzepczynski is nicknamed after what game?

★ ★ ★ ★ ★ ★ ★ ★ ★ ★ ★ ★ ★ ★ ★ ★

424) What baseball player was nicknamed D-Train?

★ ★ ★ ★ ★ ★ ★ ★ ★ ★ ★ ★ ★ ★ ★ ★

425) What actor, best known for westerns, was nicknamed the Duke?

426) Charles Addams: Cartoonist or signer of the Declaration of Independence?

★ ★ ★ ★ ★ ★ ★ ★ ★ ★ ★ ★ ★ ★ ★ ★ ★

427) John Stuart Mill: Political philosopher or Broadway actor?

★ ★ ★ ★ ★ ★ ★ ★ ★ ★ ★ ★ ★ ★ ★ ★ ★

428) PAT GARRETT: COLLEGE BASKETBALL COACH OR KILLER OF BILLY THE KID?

★ ★ ★ ★ ★ ★ ★ ★ ★ ★ ★ ★ ★ ★ ★ ★ ★

429) August Wilson: Playwright or creator of the standardized calendar.

★ ★ ★ ★ ★ ★ ★ ★ ★ ★ ★ ★ ★ ★ ★ ★

430) Marcel Duchamp: Artist or French prime minister?

★ ★ ★ ★ ★ ★ ★ ★ ★ ★ ★ ★ ★ ★ ★ ★ ★

431) Ned Kelly: Australian outlaw or Texas governor?

★ ★ ★ ★ ★ ★ ★ ★ ★ ★ ★ ★ ★ ★ ★ ★ ★

432) Henry Highland Garnet: Abolitionist or New York mayor?

433) George Best: British soccer star or "fifth Beatle"?

434) Madame C.J. Walker: Hair care entrepreneur or World War II historian?

* * * * * * * * * * * * * * *

435) DOUGLAS WILDER: VIRGINIA GOVERNOR OR INVENTOR OF THE MICROWAVE?

* * * * * * * * * * * * * * * *

436) Ambrose Burnside: Civil War general or New England poet?

* *

437) Henrik Ibsen: Inventor of the crayon or playwright.

* * * * * * * * * * * * * * *

438) Joseph Lister: Dictionary developer or founder of antiseptic medicine?

* * * * * * * * * * * * * * *

439) Modest Mussorgsky: Early fashion model or composer?

* * * * * * * * * * * * * * * * * *

440) Thomas Nast: Illustrator or adventurer?

* * * * * * * * * * * * * * * *

441) Geraldo Rivera: Motel owner or TV talk-show host?

442) WILHELM CONRAD RONTGEN: X-RAY PIONEER OR SOVIET PRISONER/AUTHOR?

****

443) Margaret Mead: Ethnologist or inventor of Jell-O?

444) Donald Neilson: *Saturday Night Live* **regular or armed robber?**

445) Brian Jones: Rolling Stones guitarist or member of Monty Python's Flying Circus?

****

446) David Koresh: **Cult leader or Internet pioneer?**

****

447) Hal Roach: Movie producer or drug lord?

****

448) Sergey Brin: Cofounder of Google or "Barbarian of Serbia"?

449) JOHN GOTTI: MOBSTER OR LOS ANGELES MAYOR?

450) Anna Quindlen: Columnist/novelist or infomercial spokesperson?

451) Jeff Bezos: **Amazon.com founder or early TV clown?**

452) Bobby Fischer: Kennedy relative or chess champion?

453) Brian Wilson: **Leader of Irish revolutionary organization or leader of the Beach Boys?**

454) Judith Jamison: Dancer/choreographer or candy manufacturer?

455) Ian Fleming: James Bond author or inventor of the nasal strip?

456) Pierre Omidyar: Middle Eastern political leader or founder of eBay?

457) Lon Chaney: Olympic wrestler or horror movie star?

458) Sam Kinison: Comedian or early motion-picture pioneer?

459) Gareth Edwards: Rugby player or modern dancer?

460) KEN FOLLETT: SPORTS ANNOUNCER OR BESTSELLING NOVELIST?

461) Tina Weymouth: Bass player/ Talking Heads cofounder or Prime Minster of England

462) Steve Allen: Original host of *The Tonight Show* or World Series of Poker champion?

463) ELIZABETH ARDEN: PRINCIPAL IN THE MOVIE *GREASE* OR BEAUTY INDUSTRY PIONEER?

464) Rowan Atkinson: Mr. Bean alter ego or founder of Bloomingdale's?

465) Shirley Bassey: Singer or congresswoman?

466) Barbara Billingsley: Creator of the Post-It note or 50s TV mom?

467) Victor Borge: Pianist or Antarctic explorer?

468) Carla Bruni: Mobster or model/First Lady of France?

469) Stephen Decatur: War of 1812 naval officer or founder of Illinois?

470) HANK GREENBERG: BASEBALL PLAYER OR CREATOR OF THE SNICKERS BAR?

471) Gene **Krupa**: Track and field star or drummer?

472) **Hugh Lofting**: *Dr. Doolittle* writer or star of *House*?

473) Nancy Lopez: **Golfer or New Mexico congresswoman?**

474) **Tom Mix: Animal rights activist or movie cowboy?**

475) James Edward Oglehorpe: Founder of Savannah, Georgia, or conflicted Wall Street inside trader?

476) **Barry Goldwater: Conservative political icon or steamboat inventor?**

CHAPTER

8

★ ★ ★ ★ ★ ★ ★ ★ ★ ★ ★

Music

477) True or false: **Paul McCartney's actual first name is James.**

* * * * * * * * * * * * * * *

478) TRUE OR FALSE: ABBA, REPRESENTING SWEDEN, WON THE EUROVISION SONG CONTEST IN 1974.

* * * * * * * * * * * * * * * *

479) True or false: **One of the members of the band Fleetwood Mac is named Fleetwood.**

* * * * * * * * * * * * * * * * * *

480) True or false: **One of the members of the band Fleetwood Mac is named Mac.**

* * * * * * * * * * * * * *

481) True or false: The Beatles were once called the Quarrymen.

* * * * * * * * * * * * * *

482) **True or false: Led Zeppelin was once called the Mugwumps.**

483) Which Beatles song came first, "Yellow Submarine" or "I Wanna Hold Your Hand"?

* *

484) True or false: In April of 1964, the Beatles had songs in all the top eight spots on the Billboard Hot 100 chart.

* * * * * * *

485) TRUE OR FALSE: THE FIRST ALBUM RELEASED ON CD WAS BY BEETHOVEN.

* * * * * * *

486) Which of the Monkees resisted any reunion tours?

a) Micky b) Michael c) Davy d) Peter

* * * * * * * * * * * * * * * * *

487) Which of the following was not a song on Kelly Clarkson's *Thankful* album?

a) "Miss Independent"   b) "Low"
c) "A Moment Like This"   d) "Never Before"

488) Which of the following was not a song on the Train album *Train*?

    a) "Meet Virginia" b) "I Am"

    c) "Iowa"   d) "Free"

489) Who sang "I Want to be Sedated" (1978)?

490) Who sang "Let's Stay Together" (1971)?

****

491) Who sang "Breathe" (2000)?

****

492) THE ROLLING STONES, THE BEATLES, THE DOORS, OR THE WHO: "HELLO, I LOVE YOU."

In an orchestra, are each of the following to the conductor's left or right?

    493) First violins   494) Cellos
    495) Violas   496) Second violins

497) True or false: In an orchestra, the tuba is positioned behind the violins.

498) True or false: In an orchestra, the harp is positioned behind the bass clarinet and in front of the percussion.

499) Which was invented first, the accordion or the saxophone?

500) Which of the following has recorded "Silent Night"?
a) Elvis Presley   b) Christina Aguilera
c) Mariah Carey   d) All of the above

501) IN "THE 12 DAYS OF CHRISTMAS," WHAT IS THE NEW ITEM GIVEN ON THE SIXTH DAY?

502) In "The 12 Days of Christmas," what are the people given on the eighth day doing?

503) In "The 12 Days of Christmas," what are the people given on the eleventh day doing?

504) True or false: According to the 2010 Christmas Price Index, the cumulative cost of all of the goods and services in "The 12 Days of Christmas" was over $23,000.

505) True or false: "Up on the House Top" is considered the first holiday song to focus on Santa.

Fill in the numeric blank in these song titles.

506) "Tea for _____"

507) "___ Tears"

508) "____ Luftballoons"

509) "_____ Spanish Angels"

• •

510) "Pennsylvania 6-_____"

a) Two   b) 96   c) 99   d) Seven   e) 5000

• •

511) TRUE OR FALSE: "DOG DAYS ARE OVER" IS ON FLORENCE AND THE MACHINE'S "CEREMONIALS" ALBUM?

• •

512) True or false: Mos Def is actually deaf.

• •

513) Do the words "piece of pie" appear in the Stone Temple Pilots song "Piece of Pie"?

• •

514) Are the Goonies mentioned in the Cyndi Lauper song "The Goonies R Good Enough"?

515) True or false: Francis Scott Key was a prisoner of war when he wrote "The Star Spangled Banner."

516) True or false: As a lawyer, Francis Scott Key successfully prosecuted Richard Lawrence, the first man to ever try to assassinate a U.S. president.

517) True or false: Francis Scott Key and author F. Scott Fitzgerald were distant cousins.

518) TRUE OR FALSE: FRANCIS SCOTT KEY IS NOT IN THE SONGWRITERS HALL OF FAME.

519) How high up the Billboard Hot 100 chart did Whitney Houston's 1983 version of "The Star Spangled Banner" climb?
a) Number 6   b) Number 12
c) Number 20   d) Number 40

520) Which comedienne stirred up controversy when she spit after singing "The Star Spangled Banner" at a Padres baseball game?
a) Lucille Ball   b) Roseanne Barr
c) Phyllis Diller   d) Sarah Silverman

521) When did Jimi Hendrix begin performing his electric guitar version of "The Star Spangled Banner"?
a) 1964   b) 1966
c) 1968   d) 1970

522) **True or false:** There is only one verse to "The Star Spangled Banner."

523) True or false: "Angels We Have Heard on High" is based on a French carol.

524) In "Angels We Have Heard on High," what are the angels singing o'er?

525) "AWAY IN A MANGER" WAS FIRST PUBLISHED IN 1885 IN...
A) PHILADELPHIA   B) LONDON
C) PARIS   D) ROME

526) True or false: "Decks the Halls" was originally called "Deck the Hall."

527) According to "Deck the Halls," what should you join after striking the harp?

528) True or false: As recorded by SHeDAISY, "Deck the Halls" made it to number 10 on the Billboard Hot 100.

* * * * * * * * * * * * * * * * *

529) True or false: "The First Noel" was written by Irving Berlin.

* *

530) What Broadway show featured the song "Yankee Doodle Dandy"?

a) *Show Boat*

b) *Oklahoma!*

c) *1776*

d) *Little Johnny Jones*

* *

531) WHO PLAYED KRIS KRINGLE IN THE ANIMATED "SANTA CLAUS IS COMIN' TO TOWN"?

A) MICKEY MANTLE   B) MICKEY ROONEY

C) MICHAEL MURPHY   D) MITCH MILLER

532) How many times is Santa checking his list in the song "Santa Claus Is Comin' to Town"?

533) What number reindeer is Rudolph?

****
534) True or false: Gene Autry was the first to record "Rudolph the Red-nosed Reindeer."

535) David Bowie or Billy Joel: *The Rise and Fall of Ziggy Stardust and the Spiders from Mars?*

536) B.B. King or Carole King: *Tapestry?*

****
537) Led Zeppelin or Pink Floyd: *The Wall?*

****
538) BOB MARLEY OR LITTLE RICHARD: *LEGEND?*

****
539) Simon and Garfunkel or Stevie Wonder: *Songs in the Key of Life?*

540) Loretta Lynn or Bjork: *Vespertine?*

● ●

541) Radiohead or the Jayhawks: *In Rainbows?*

● ●

542) Jay-Z or Arcade Fire: *The Blueprint?*

● ●

543) Death Cab for Cutie or the Flaming Lips: *Transatlanticism?*

● ●

544) The Shins or the Decemberists: *The Crane Wife?*

● ●

545) VAMPIRE WEEKEND OR BECK: *SEA CHANGE?*

● ●

546) Rufus Wainwright or Amy Winehouse: *Back to Black?*

547) **Kanye West or Patty Griffin:** *1000 Kisses?*

548) The Avett Brothers or OutKast: *I and Love and You?*

549) **The White Stripes or Radiohead:** *Elephant?*

550) Sufjan Stevens or Wilco: *Yankee Hotel Foxtrot?*

CHAPTER

9

It Happened in . . .

1988

551) True or false: The leader of the Soviet Union in 1988 was Mikhail Gorbachev.

* *

552) WHO WAS THE VICE PRESIDENT OF THE UNITED STATES IN 1988?

* *

553) In 1988, what was Anthony M. Kennedy appointed to?

554) Where were the 1988 Winter Olympics held?
a) Soviet Union   b) Finland
c) Canada   d) United States

555) Which of the following was not a Democratic presidential candidate in 1988?
a) Jesse Jackson   b) Richard Gephardt
c) Michael Dukakis   d) Evan Mecham

* *

556) In the Hebrew calendar, it was what year in 1988?
a) 5748-5749   b) 5750-5751
c) 5752-5753   d) 5754-5755

557) What comic strip had its debut in 1988
    a) FoxTrot   b) Doonesbury
    c) B.C.   d) Hagar the Horrible

558) What film won the 1988 Oscar for Best Picture?
    a) *Rain Man*
    b) *Dangerous Liaisons*
    c) *Mississippi Burning*
    d) *The Accidental Tourist*

559) WHAT FORMER POP SINGER BECAME MAYOR OF PALM SPRINGS, CALIFORNIA?
    A) BETTE MIDLER
    B) SONNY BONO
    C) JONI MITCHELL
    D) JUDY COLLINS

****
560) Where was the 1988 World Expo held?
        a) Australia   b) Austria
        c) England   d) Egypt

561) In 1988, the Supreme Court decided that the police didn't need one of these to look through thrown-out garbage?

562) What national park faced massive wildfires in 1988?
- a) Grand Canyon
- b) Great Smokey Mountains
- c) Yellowstone
- d) Yosemite

563) Where were the 1988 Summer Olympics held?
- a) South Korea
- b) Vietnam
- c) Japan
- d) China

564) What food company did Philip Morris buy in 1988?
- a) Campbell's
- b) Kraft
- c) Kellogg's
- d) Nabisco

565) True or false: In 1988, the first computer worm was released.

566) WHO DID GEORGE H.W. BUSH DEFEAT IN THE 1988 PRESIDENTIAL ELECTION?

567) What future one-named singer was born in Barbados in 1988?

568) What future star of *Arrested Development* and *Nick and Norah's Infinite Playlist* was born in 1988?

569) What Princess of York was born in 1988?

570) What did Naguib Mahfouz win the Nobel Prize for in 1988?
   a) Medicine   b) Physics
   c) Literature   d) Peace

571) Each of these was a #1 hit for Michael Jackson in 1988 EXCEPT:
a) "Bad"
b) "Dirty Diana"
c) "The Man in the Mirror"
d) "The Way You Make Me Feel"

572) Each of these was a #1 hit for George Michael in 1988 EXCEPT:
   a) "Father Figure"   b) "Kissing a Fool"
   c) "Monkey"   d) "One More Try"

573) ONE OF THE BIGGEST HITS OF 1988, SPENDING THREE WEEKS AT #1, WAS WHAT SINGLE BY POISON?
   A) "EVERY ROSE HAS ITS THORN"
   B) "NOTHIN' BUT A GOOD TIME"
   C) "TALK DIRTY TO ME"
   D) "UNSKINNY BOP"

574) True or false: Rick Astley's "Never Gonna Give You Up" was a #1 hit in 1988.

575) Guns 'n' Roses released what album in 1988?
   a) Appetite for Destruction
   b) Destruction Zone
   c) Eve of Destruction
   d) Self-Destruction

576) Who was reelected president of France in 1988?
   a) Jacques Chirac
   b) Valery Giscard d'Estaing
   c) Francois Mitterrand
   d) Nicolas Sarkozy

577) George H.W. Bush used what three-word phrase in vowing never to raise taxes if elected president?

578) The Soviet Union began pulling troops out of what country in 1988?
a) Afghanistan   b) Angola   c) Cuba   d) Poland

579) What country ousted Janos Kadar as its leader after more than 30 years in power?
   a) Czechoslovakia   b) East Germany
   c) Hungary   d) Romania

580) AFTER EIGHT YEARS OF WAR, IRAQ AGREED TO A CEASEFIRE WITH WHAT COUNTRY?
A) IRAN   B) KUWAIT
C) SAUDI ARABIA   D) UNITED STATES

581) What country became the first Muslim nation to be governed by a woman?
a) Indonesia   b) Jordan
c) Pakistan   d) Saudi Arabia

* *

582) Who was prime minister of Canada in 1988?
a) **Kim Campbell**   b) **Jean Chretien**
c) **Brian Mulroney** d) **Pierre Trudeau**

* * * * * * * * * * * * * * * *

583) What pitcher broke a record by ending the season with 59 consecutive shutout innings?
a) Roger Clemens   b) Dennis Eckersley
c) Orel Hershiser   d) Dave Stewart

584) True or false: Kurt Vonnegut's novel *Paris Trout* was published in 1988.

585) Complete the titles of these novels published in 1988.

a) Breathing _____   1) Agenda
b) The Cardinal of the _____   2) Kremlin
c) Foucault's _____   3) Lessons
d) The Icarus _____   4) Pendulum

586) In 1988, who became the first tennis player in 18 years to win all four Grand Slam tournaments?

a) Andre Agassi   b) Stefan Edberg
c) Steffi Graf   d) Monica Seles

587) WHO WERE THE TWO STARS OF *RAIN MAN*, THE WINNER OF THE OSCAR FOR BEST PICTURE?

* *

588) Who recorded the 1988 hit song "Don't Worry, Be Happy"?

a) Bobby McFerrin
b) Bobby Brown
c) Bobby Brooks
d) Bobby Bacharach

1989

589) The Polish United Workers Party formed a labor union famously called...
a) Togetherness   b) One-for-all
c) Solidarity   d) Singleness

590) GEORGE H.W. BUSH BECAME PRESIDENT OF THE UNITED STATES, REPLACING WHO?

591) What was the name of the boat that spilled oil in the waters off Alaska?
a) Exxon Electra
b) Exxon Esso
c) Exxon Valiant
d) Exxon Valdez

592) Which park opened in Florida?
a) EPCOT
b) Disney-MGM Studios
c) Disney's Animal Kingdom
d) Universal's Island of Adventure

593) Mikhail Gorbachev became the first Soviet ruler to visit this country since the 1960s.

a) United States b) China
c) Japan   d) England

594) **What was the site of protests in China?**

a) Tiananmen Square b) Tammarind Square
c) Beijing Square   d) Dragon Square

595) What was the name of the Iranian leader who died in 1989?

a) Ayatollah Kommanchi b) Ayatollah Kampchatka
c) Ayatollah Khomeini   d) Ayatollah Karmax

596) What was the name of the hand-held system released by Nintendo in 1989?

597) WHAT SEGA SYSTEM IS RELEASED IN 1989?

598) What baseball legend was banned from the game for allegedly gambling?

599) What was the name of the Hurricane that hit South Carolina in 1989?

a) Harold   b) Hugo

c) Herman   d) Henry

600) Nicolae Ceausescu was overthrown as ruler of what country?

a) Hungary   b) Rumania

c) Turkey   d) France

★ ★ ★ ★ ★ ★ ★ ★ ★ ★ ★ ★ ★ ★ ★ ★

601) What book by Salman Rushdie led to Iran's leader putting a bounty on him?

a) *The Satanic Purses*

b) *The Satanic Nurses*

c) *The Satanic Verses*

d) *The Satanic Curses*

★ ★ ★ ★ ★ ★ ★ ★ ★ ★ ★ ★ ★ ★ ★ ★

602) Who was convicted in what was known as the Iran-Contra Affair?

a) Oliver West   b) Oliver East

c) Oliver South   d) Oliver North

603) What was the cost of a first-class stamp in 1989?

604) WHAT RACE DID SUNDAY SILENCE WIN IN 1989?

★ ★ ★ ★ ★ ★ ★ ★ ★ ★ ★ ★ ★ ★ ★ ★ ★

605) What was the name of the star of *I Love Lucy* who died in 1989?

★ ★ ★ ★ ★ ★ ★ ★ ★ ★ ★ ★ ★ ★ ★ ★ ★

606) What show won the Emmy Award for Outstanding Drama in 1989?
a) *St. Elsewhere*   b) *L.A. Law*
c) *NYPD Blue*   d) *Law and Order*

607) Who was the great Shakespearian actor who died in 1989?
a) John Barrymore   b) Laurence Olivier
c) Edwin Booth   d) Marie Iaconangelo

608) Which Jackson had a #1 hit in 1989, Janet or Michael?

★ ★ ★ ★ ★ ★ ★ ★ ★ ★ ★ ★ ★ ★ ★ ★ ★

609) What future TV personality had three #1 hits in 1989?

★ ★ ★ ★ ★ ★ ★ ★ ★ ★ ★ ★ ★ ★ ★ ★ ★

610) What duo had three #1 hits in 1989, but were stripped of the Best New Artist Grammy for the year after it turned out they'd been lip-syncing?

611) WHICH COUNTRY WAS THE FIRST TO BREAK FREE FROM THE COMMUNIST BLOC?

    A) EAST GERMANY   B) HUNGARY

    C) LITHUANIA   D) POLAND

* *

612) What monarch died after 62 years on the throne?

a) King Abdullah   b) Queen Beatrix

c) Emperor Hirohito   d) King Hussein

* *

613) Cuban troops began a withdrawal from what nation in 1989?

    a) Angola   b) El Salvador

    c) Haiti   d) Mozambique

* *

    614) Donald Trump bought the landing rights to operate a New York–to–Washington and New York–to–Boston air shuttle from what struggling airline?

    a) Eastern   b) Northwest

    c) Southwest   d) Western

* * * * * * * * * * * *

615) What was torn down, beginning on November 9?

616) Alfredo Stroessner was overthrown after 35 years as the dictator of what country?
- a) Austria
- b) East Germany
- c) Liechtenstein
- d) Paraguay

617) U.S. troops invaded what nation in December, forcing out the country's president seven months after he ignored his loss in national elections?
- a) Grenada
- b) Haiti
- c) Nicaragua
- d) Panama

618) WHO BECAME NEW YORK CITY'S FIRST AFRICAN-AMERICAN MAYOR?
- A) DAVID DINKINS
- B) CARL MCCALL
- C) DAVID PATERSON
- D) ADAM CLAYTON POWELL

619) Bristol-Myers merged with what pharmaceutical company?
- a) Lilly
- b) Merck
- c) Squibb
- d) Wyeth

620) The House passed, but the Senate rejected, a constitutional amendment to overturn a Supreme Court decision allowing what?

a) Free cigarettes   b) Flag burning

c) Gerrymandering   d) School prayer

• •

621) Match the notable books of 1989 to their authors.

a) *Billy Bathgate*   1) Stephen Covey

b) *The Dark Half*   2) E.L. Doctorow

c) *The Joy Luck Club*   3) John Grisham

d) *A Prayer for Owen Meany*   4) John Irving

e) *The Remains of the Day*   5) Kazuo Ishiguro

f) *The Russia House*   6) Stephen King

g) *The Seven Habits of*   7) John le Carre

   Highly Effective People   8) Amy Tan

h) *A Time to Kill*

• •

622) The Corcoran Gallery in Washington canceled a planned exhibition of the works of what controversial photographer?

• •

623) George Harrison, Bob Dylan, Roy Orbison, Tom Petty, and Jeff Lynne united to form what supergroup?

624) What interrupted the World Series for 11 days?
a) Earthquake   b) Flooding   c) Hurricane   d) Rioting

625) What televangelist was sentenced to 45 years in prison for fraud?
   a) Benny Hinn   b) Oral Roberts
   c) Jimmy Swaggart   d) Jim Bakker

626) TRUE OR FALSE: THE ACTOR WHO PLAYED SHOELESS JOE JACKSON IN *FIELD OF DREAMS* PLAYED MINOR-LEAGUE BALL IN THE CHICAGO WHITE SOX SYSTEM.

627) William Bennett became the first person to hold what U.S. government post?
   a) Drug czar
   b) Secretary of Education
   c) Secretary of Energy
   d) Secretary of Homeland Security

628) What hotelier was dubbed "The Queen of Mean" during her trial for tax evasion?
a) Lori Partridge   b) Leona Helmsley
c) Lisa Birnbaum   d) Leslie Stahl

629) What party gave up exclusive rule of the Soviet Union in 1990?
   a) Democratic Party
   b) Socialist Party
   c) Communist Party
   d) Whig Party

630) WHO WAS FREED IN SOUTH AFRICA AFTER MORE THAN 27 YEARS IN PRISON?

631) What country did Iraq invade in 1990, starting the Persian Gulf War?
   a) Egypt   b) Israel
   c) Sudan   d) Kuwait

632) Did Margaret Thatcher resign and John Major become British Prime Minster or vice versa?

633) Who was the vice president of the U.S. in 1990?

634) What West Coast team beat Denver in the 1990 Super Bowl 55-10?

635) Who won in the Men's Wimbledon battle between Stefan Edberg and Boris Becker?

636) The X-rating for movies was replaced by what rating in 1990?

637) WHAT LONG RUNNING ANIMATED TV SERIES LAUNCHED ON FOX IN 1990?

638) What show business magazine began publishing in 1990?
a) *Entertainment Weekly*
b) *Variety*
c) *The Hollywood Reporter*
d) *TV Guide*

639) What was the name of the Muppet creator who died in 1990?

640) What Washington D.C. landmark was completed in 1990?
a) The Smithsonian Air and Space Museum
b) The National Gallery of Art
c) The National Cathedral
d) The Vietnam Veterans Memorial

641) What singer began her career with five straight #1 hits, with the first two topping the charts in 1990?

a) Mariah Carey   **b) Paula Cole**

c) Melissa Etheridge   **d) Whitney Houston**

* * * * * * * * * * * * * * *

642) Robert Van Winkle topped the charts under what stage name?
a) Gino Vannelli   b) Milli Vanilli
c) Vanilla Fudge   d) Vanilla Ice

643) Alannah Myles' single "Black Velvet" is about whom?
a) James Brown b) Michael Jackson
c) Elvis Presley d) Barry White

644) MICHAEL BOLTON RE-RECORDED "HOW AM I SUPPOSED TO LIVE WITHOUT YOU?" AND TOOK IT TO #1, SEVEN YEARS AFTER WRITING IT FOR WHAT SINGER?

A) LAURA BRANIGAN   B) JANET JACKSON

C) JOAN JETT   D) DOLLY PARTON

* *

645) Kevin Costner won an Oscar for 1990's Dances With Wolves. In what category?
a) Best Actor
b) Best Director
c) Best Original Score
d) Best Original Screenplay

* * * * * * * * * * * * * * *

646) What was the biggest box-office hit of 1990?
a) *Dances With Wolves*
b) *Ghost*
c) *Home Alone*
d) *Total Recall*

MAYBE WE SHOULD RE-THINK THE TITLE OF THIS MOVIE!

DANCES WITH BISON

647) "It Must Have Been Love" was a #1 hit off the soundtrack of what 1990 romantic comedy?

648) What 1965 hit by the Righteous Brothers reentered the Top 20 in 1990, thanks to its use in the movie Ghost?
- a) "Rock and Roll Heaven"
- b) "Soul and Inspiration"
- c) "Unchained Melody"
- d) "You've Lost That Lovin' Feeling"

649) Who starred in two of the ten biggest box office hits of 1990?
- a) Harrison Ford
- b) Richard Gere
- c) Arnold Schwarzenegger
- d) Bruce Willis

650) What creator of Willy Wonka died in 1990?

651) Match the author to his 1990 work.
- a) *Hocus Pocus*
- b) *An Inconvenient Woman*
- c) *Jurassic Park*
- d) *Vineland*

652) WHAT TALK SHOW HOST GUEST-HOSTED *THE PAT SAJAK SHOW* IN 1990, AND HAD TO CLEAR THE STUDIO AFTER A PROLONGED ON-AIR ARGUMENT WITH ABORTION-RIGHTS AND GAY-RIGHTS ACTIVISTS IN THE AUDIENCE?

A) GLENN BECK   B) SEAN HANNITY

C) RUSH LIMBAUGH   D) BILL O'REILLY

653) **Who created the TV series *Twin Peaks*, which debuted in 1990?**

654) On Twin Peaks, who killed Laura Palmer?

a) Her boyfriend   b) Her father

c) Her mother   d) Windom Earle

655) True or false: **East and West Germany united in 1990.**

656) True or false: **North and South Yemen united in 1990.**

657) True or false: North and South Vietnam united in 1990.

658) TRUE OR FALSE: NORTH AND SOUTH SUDAN UNITED IN 1990.

659) True or false: North and South Korea united in 1990.

660) True or false: **East and West Pakistan united in 1990.**

661) General Motors introduced what ultimately unsuccessful car in 1990?
a) Chevette b) Saturn c) Trabant d) Volt

662) A 15-year civil war in what country ended in 1990?
a) Iran   b) Iraq
c) Lebanon   d) Qatar

663) What African nation declared independence in 1990?
a) Congo   b) Liberia   c) Namibia   d) Zambia

664) Michael Milken, who went to prison for insider trading in 1990, pioneered the trading of what financial instrument?
a) Credit-default swaps
b) Derivatives
c) Junk bonds
d) Mortgage-based bonds

665) WHAT WAS BANNED ON U.S. AIRLINE FLIGHTS IN 1990?

A) CELL PHONES

B) LIQUIDS

C) WEAPONS

D) SMOKING

666) *Entertainment Weekly* made its debut in 1990, with whom on the cover?
a) Mia Farrow
b) Whitney Houston
c) k.d. lang
d) Oprah Winfrey

667) Which man was **NOT** heavyweight champion of the world for part of 1990?
a) Buster Douglas
b) George Foreman
c) Evander Holyfield
d) Mike Tyson

668) What country won the 1990 World Cup?
a) Argentina
b) Brazil
c) France
d) Germany

1991

669) Who became the first freely elected president of the Russian Republic?
a) Georgy Malenkov
b) Alexei Kosygin
c) Leonid Brezhnev
d) Boris Yeltsin

* * * * * * * * * * * * * *

670) Who won the Duke vs. Kansas NCAA Basketball Championship in 1991?

* *

671) What Seattle band released the song "Smells Like Teen Spirit"?

* *

672) In 1991, a nuclear accident happened in what country?
a) United States   b) China
c) Yugoslavia   d) Japan

* *

673) What airline shut down in 1991?
a) TWA   b) Pan-Am
c) Eastern d) American TransAir

674) What cable channel launched in 1991 after the merger of two rival channels, the Comedy Channel and Ha!?

• •

675) IN 1991, AN ATTENDEE OF WHAT MAJOR SPORTING EVENT WAS KILLED BY LIGHTNING?
A) SUPER BOWL   B) WORLD SERIES
C) U.S. OPEN   D) KENTUCKY DERBY

* *

676) Which one dissolved in 1991 to be replaced by the other: The Supreme Soviet of the Soviet Union or the Congress of People's Deputies of the Soviet Union.

• •

677) Which of the following did not declare independence in 1991 after the dissolution of the Soviet Union?
a) Azerbaijan   b) Kyrgyzstan
c) Stanicole   d) Moldova

* *

678) What Governor of Arkansas declared his intentions of running for President?

• •

679) What L.A. Lakers star announced that he had H.I.V.?

680) What legendary jazz trumpeter, composer, and bandleader died in 1991?
a) Charles Mingus b) Miles Davis
c) Duke Ellington   d) Louis Armstrong

681) WHAT SONG FROM THE *ROBIN HOOD: PRINCE OF THIEVES* SOUNDTRACK WAS THE BIGGEST HIT OF 1991, SPENDING SEVEN WEEKS AT #1?

682) True or false: Michael Jackson had his final #1 hit in 1991 with "Black or White."

683) What is the title of the #1 hit subtitled "Everybody Dance Now"?

684) What Christian contemporary act's biggest mainstream hit was 1991's "Baby Baby"?
a) Amy Grant   b) Petra
c) Michael W. Smith   d) Stryper

685) Germany moved its capital to Berlin from what city in 1991?

686) In the last gasp of the Soviet Union, Soviet troops staged a violent crackdown in what breakaway Baltic republic?

a) Estonia   b) Georgia   c) Latvia   d) Lithuania

687) What code name was given to the invasion of Iraq?
- a) Operation Barbarossa
- b) Operation Desert Storm
- c) Operation Enduring Freedom
- d) Operation Overlord

688) WHO STARRED IN TWO OF THE TOP TEN MONEYMAKING MOVIES OF 1991?

A) KEVIN COSTNER   B) ANTHONY HOPKINS

C) ARNOLD SCHWARZENEGGER   D) ROBIN WILLIAMS

689) *The Silence of the Lambs* won Oscars in each of these categories
EXCEPT:
- a) Best Picture
- b) Best Actress
- c) Best Supporting Actor
- d) Best Director

I'D LIKE TO THANK THE ACADEMY...

690) Who began a 17-year run as host of Meet the Press in 1991?

691) What game show, which debuted in 1991, put young contestants in charge of tracking villains such as Sarah Nade and Patty Larceny?
a) *Brain Surge*
b) *Double Dare*
c) *Where in the World is Carmen Sandiego?*
d) *You Can't Do That on Television*

692) Whose missed field goal decided Super Bowl XXV?

693) What team defeated the Buffalo Bills in Super Bowl XXV?
a) Green Bay Packers   b) New York Giants
c) San Francisco 49ers   d) Tampa Bay Buccaneers

694) A 1991 Douglas Coupland book coined what term for the generation that followed the Baby Boomers?

1992

695) WHERE WAS PRESIDENT BUSH WHEN HE THREW UP ON CAMERA AT A STATE DINNER?

A) WASHINGTON, D.C.

B) JAPAN

C) CHINA

D) MEXICO

696) When the artists' boycott of South Africa ended, who was the first major musician to tour there?

a) Bruce Springsteen   b) Bono

c) Paul Simon   d) Elton John

697) The 1992 Winter Olympics were held in Albertville...

a) France   b) Germany   c) Italy   d) Greece

698) Which Disney park opened in 1992?

a) Disneyland Tokyo

b) EPCOT

c) Euro Disneyland

d) No Disney park opened in 1992

699) Riots caused death and damage in L.A. after four police officers were acquitted in the beating of who?

a) Rodney Allen Ripey   b) Rodney King
c) Rodney Dangerfield   d) Rodney Reynolds

700) WHAT MONETARY UNIT REPLACED THE RUBLE IN ESTONIA?

A) THE KRUPA   B) THE KROON

C) THE CARROT D) THE KLAM

* *

701) Singer Sinead O'Conner caused controversy when she tore up a photo of

who while she was a musical guest on *Saturday Night Live?*

a) Ronald Reagan
b) Pope John Paul II
c) Muhammad
d) Madonna

* *

702) In 1992, Bill Clinton was elected the _____ President of the United States.

a) 39th   b) 40th   c) 41st   d) 42nd

* *

703) Who did Princess Diana separate from in 1992?

704) What famous music hall in Paris, France, closed in 1992?

a) The Sorbonne   b) The Follies Bergere

c) The Ritz   d) Minsky's

* *

705) What *Twilight* actor was born in February of 1992?

706) John Cage died in 1992. What was Cage best known as?

a) Basketball player   b) Politician

c) Zookeeper   d) Composer

707) ANTHONY PERKINS DIED IN 1992. WHAT HORROR MOVIE WAS HE MOST FAMOUS FOR APPEARING IN?

A) *A NIGHTMARE ON ELM STREET*

B) *PSYCHO*

C) *HALLOWEEN*

D) *FRIDAY THE 13TH*

* *

708) *Unforgiven* won Best Picture at the Oscars. What kind of film was it?

a) Musical   b) Comedy

c) Romantic drama   d) Western

ANSWERS

1) c
2) b
3) a
4) d
5) Parental Guidance Suggested
6) *The Wrath of Khan, The Search for Spock, The Voyage Home, The Final Frontier, The Undiscovered Country.*
7) six
8) the movie
9) true
10) a. *Usher,* b. *Now,* c. *World,* d. *Music,* e. *Apes,* f. *Men,* g. *Tap,* h. *Night,* i. *Hood,* j. *Black*
11) false
12) four
13) *Superman Returns*
14) a
15) true
16) Jim Carrey
17) true
18) a. *Sharpay's Fabulous Adventure,* b. *Lemonade Mouth,* c. *My Babysitter's a Vampire,* d. *Camp Rock 2: The Final Jam,* e. *Princess Protection Program,* f. *The Cheetah Girls: One World,* g. *Minutemen,* h. *Wendy Wu: Homecoming Warrior,* i. *High School Musical,* j. *Stuck in the Suburbs*
19) *H.R. Pufnstuf*
20) Miss Frizzle
21) *Beverly Hills 90210* (296)
22) d
23) false
24) true
25) true
26) Home Box Office
27) Home & Garden Television
28) Do-it-yourself Network
29) *Lassie* (588)
30) a. 10, b. 4, c. 7, d. 5, e. 2, f. 3, g. 9, h. 1, i. 6, j. 8
31) Leo Durocher
32) Washington
33) St. Louis
34) Kansas City
35) c
36) a
37) d

38) true
39) 6
40) a. 3, b. 2, c. 4, d. 1
41) false—but was true
    in 1920, when he
    hit 54
42) c
43) false
44) false
45) b
46) d
47) a
48) false
49) no
50) no
51) yes
52) yes
53) no
54) no
55) no
56) no
57) yes
58) yes
59) Jim Brown
60) Baltimore Ravens
61) b
62) Heisman Trophy
63) d
64) a
65) d
66) true
67) true
68) false—a soccer ball

69) true
70) true
71) Los Angeles Lakers
72) less
73) b
74) true
75) yes—Frank Selvy for
    Furman University
76) true
77) true
78) true
79) b
80) false—19 ft. 9 inches
81) c
82) true—Cincinnatus
    Powell, who played
    1967-1975
83) yes
84) France
85) false
86) false—in 1991
87) false—he was 17
88) yes—Brazil vs.
    Sweden
89) false—40 years old
90) false—there's one
    referee and two
    linesmen
91) b
92) c
93) no
94) 300
95) a 7-10 split

96) 4-6-7-10
97) three
98) true
99) true
100) a
101) true
102) c
103) b
104) c
105) true
106) a
107) true
108) apples
109) pears
110) grapes
111) bananas
112) mango
113) bananas
114) false—usually soup
    is the only liquid
115) true
116) b
117) Kellogg's
118) b
119) Alpha-bits
120) Apple Jacks
121) *The Simpsons*
122) c
123) false—there was
    a Whaler and
    an Ocean Catch
    sandwich, but no
    Big Swimmer

124) true
125) Burger King
126) b
127) true
128) Japan
129) false—McDonald's
    did try suing, but
    the word still went
    in
130) true
131) Subway
132) true
133) *Treasure Island*
134) false— it owns
    Donato's
135) false
136) d
137) d
138) b
139) Independence Day
140) forty-three
141) ten minutes
142) yes
143) separately
144) Coney Island, New
    York
145) a
146) false—it stands for
    owner Paul Fleming
147) true
148) true
149) c
150) the tomato sauce

151) a
152) true
153) false—cheese is
154) October
155) true—Europeans later
added tomatoes
156) false—peanuts
157) Mr. Goodbar
158) three
159) red
160) s'mores
161) true
162) true—as long as it
has less than .5
grams per serving
163) true
164) salt
165) d
166) air
167) true
168) true
169) 7-Up
170) false
171) d
172) U.S.A.
173) j
174) true
175) center of the board
176) dark
177) no
178) c
179) b
180) false

181) false
182) true
183) two
184) Showdown Yahtzee
185) true
186) false—it's called a
prime
187) true
188) no
189) b—the category is
Data Head
190) one minute
191) true
192) b
193) a
194) b
195) b
196) fifty
197) false—they are made
from Vermont maple
198) true
199) three
200) b—because there is
only one z
201) Asia
202) d
203) eight
204) $100,000
205) d
206) a
207) $2 million
208) true
209) false

210) top hat
211) two
212) twelve
213) two
214) true
215) $200
216) false
217) New York Avenue
218) false
219) $1,500
220) Park Place
221) false—that's Luxury Tax
222) c
223) Pacific Avenue
224) Kentucky Avenue
225) St. James Avenue
226) c
227) across
228) true
229) the answer is in abbreviated form
230) to the second highest ranking
231) no
232) no—it has to be completely in the numbered area
233) three
234) one
235) last
236) yes
237) a

238) any part of is has to be six inches from the stake.
239) One
240) c
241) true
242) d
243) a
244) c
245) b
246) d
247) c
248) b
249) a
250) false—the number ranges from 4,500-5,000
251) Warm-blooded
252) f
253) e
254) d
255) a
256) b
257) c
258) false
259) back—it's got four on each front foot and five on each back
260) yes
261) true
262) false—its hair thins out over time, leaving patches of skin

263) true
264) false—it's always white-tipped
265) true
266) four
267) American
268) true
269) true
270) true
271) true
272) false—they are curved
273) false—they are about the same size
274) fore claws
275) false
276) a black bear
277) five
278) false—they grow slowly through its lifetime
279) black bear
280) Kodiak—It can reach over 12 feet on its hind legs
281) false
282) false
283) true
284) c
285) true
286) no—it's black
287) yes
288) hare
289) true
290) true
291) true
292) false
293) true
294) cheetah
295) black
296) false
297) true
298) smaller
299) c
300) Asian
301) false
302) b
303) false—they are at the end of its snout
304) false
305) false
306) male
307) yes
308) b
309) a
310) false—they are only slightly longer
311) b
312) c
313) Detective Comics
314) Mandrake
315) true
316) false—it happened in the 1940s
317) d
318) false

319) b
320) true
321) true
322) b
323) Alan Moore's
    Watchmen
324) true—Gene Yang's
    *American Born
    Chinese*
325) c
326) false—more like 200
327) true
328) b
329) true
330) c
331) Marvel
332) DC
333) DC
334) Marvel
335) DC
336) Marvel
337) True—1940
338) Human Torch
339) b
340) he can stretch his
    body
341) invisibility
342) Human Torch
343) the Thing
344) a. 8, b. 7, c. 9, d. 1,
    e. 3, f. 10, g. 4,
    h. 5, i. 6, j. 2
345) c

346) a
347) a
348) b
349) a
350) Jughead
351) Veronica
352) true
353) Riverdale
354) drums
355) false—her name was
    Forsythia
356) c
357) true
358) true
359) b
360) b
361) Jon
362) Odie
363) d
364) false
365) Charlie Brown
366) Van Pelt
367) Rerun
368) Chuck
369) blonde
370) catcher
371) false—he's a barber
372) a girl
373) false
374) the Red Baron
375) Sopwith Camel
376) Lady Gaga
377) Kirk Douglas

378) true
379) true
380) Diane Keaton
381) Joan Rivers
382) false—it's actress
    Lauren Bacall
383) d
384) c
385) b
386) a
387) false—she has no
    middle name
388) Billy the Kid
389) Mark Twain
390) British prime
    minister
391) head of Pixar
392) CIA director
393) Irish resistance
    leader
394) Chilean writer
395) humor writer
396) magazine editor
397) Survivor producer
398) pianist
399) historian
400) folk singer
401) first woman to
    graduate from
    medical school
402) gorilla researcher
403) no
404) no

405) yes
406) no
407) yes
408) no
409) no
410) yes
411) yes
412) yes
413) yes
414) yes
415) no
416) yes
417) yes
418) Alex Rodriguez
419) Francisco Rodriguez
420) Tracy McGrady
421) Joseph Burnett
422) Kenyon Martin
423) Scrabble
424) Dontrelle Willis
425) John Wayne
426) cartoonist
427) political
philosopher
428) killer of Billy the
    Kid
429) playwright
430) artist
431) Australian outlaw
432) abolitionist
433) British soccer star
434) hair care
    entrepreneur

435) Virginia governor
436) Civil War general
437) playwright
438) founder of antiseptic medicine
439) composer
440) illustrator
441) TV talk-show host
442) X-ray pioneer
443) ethnologist
444) armed robber
445) Rolling Stones guitarist
446) cult leader
447) movie producer
448) cofounder of Google
449) mobster
450) columnist/novelist
451) Amazon.com founder
452) chess champion
453) leader of the Beach Boys
454) dancer/choreographer
455) James Bond author
456) founder of eBay
457) horror movie star
458) comedian
459) rugby player
460) bestselling novelist
461) bass player/Talking Heads cofounder
462) original host of *The Tonight Show*
463) beauty industry pioneer
464) Mr. Bean alter ego
465) singer
466) 50s TV mom
467) pianist
468) model/First Lady of France
469) War of 1812 naval officer
470) baseball player
471) drummer
472) *Dr. Doolittle* writer
473) golfer
474) movie cowboy
475) founder of Savannah, Georgia
476) conservative political icon
477) true
478) true
479) true—Mick Fleetwood
480) false
481) true
482) false
483) "I Wanna Hold Your Hand"
484) false—"only" the top five
485) false—It was Billy Joel's *52nd Street*
486) b

487) d
488) c
489) The Ramones
490) Al Green
491) Faith Hill
492) The Doors
493) left
494) right
495) right
496) left
497) false
498) true
499) accordion
500) d
501) geese-a-laying
502) milking
503) piping
504) true
505) true
506) a
507) b
508) c
509) d
510) e
511) false
512) false
513) no
514) no
515) false
516) true
517) true
518) false—He was
    inducted in 1970

519) c
520) b
521) c
522) false
523) true
524) the plains
525) a
526) true
527) the chorus
528) false—It only made
    it to 61
529) false—it's a
    traditional English
    carol
530) d
531) b
532) twice
533) nine
534) false
535) David Bowie
536) Carole King
537) Pink Floyd
538) Bob Marley
539) Stevie Wonder
540) Bjork
541) Radiohead
542) Jay-Z
543) Death Cab for Cutie
544) The Decemberists
545) Beck
546) Amy Winehouse
547) Patty Griffin
548) The Avett Brothers

549) The White Stripes
550) Wilco
551) true
552) George H.W. Bush
553) The Supreme Court
554) c
555) d
556) a
557) a
558) a
559) b
560) a
561) search warrant
562) c
563) a
564) b
565) true
566) Michael Dukakis
567) Rihanna
568) Michael Cera
569) Beatrice
570) c
571) a
572) b
573) a
574) true
575) a
576) c
577) read my lips
578) a
579) c
580) a
581) c

582) c
583) c
584) false—it's by Pete Dexter
585) a 3, b 2, c 4, d a
586) c
587) Tom Cruise and Dustin Hoffman
588) a
589) c
590) Ronald Reagan
591) d
592) b
593) b
594) a
595) c
596) Game Boy
597) Genesis
598) Pete Rose
599) b
600) b
601) c
602) d
603) a quarter
604) Kentucky Derby
605) Lucille Ball
606) b
607) b
608) Janet
609) Paula Abdul
610) Milli Vanilli
611) d
612) c

613) a
614) a
615) the Berlin Wall
616) d
617) d
618) a
619) c
620) b
621) a 2, b 6, c 8, d 4,
   e 5, f 7, g 1, h 3
622) Robert Mapplethorpe
623) the Traveling
   Wilburys
624) a
625) d
626) false—though a
   namesake and
   relative of actor Ray
   Liotta did
627) a
628) b
629) c
630) Nelson Mandela
631) d
632) Thatcher resigned/
   Major became Prime
   Minister
633) J. Danforth Quayle
634) San Francisco 49ers
635) Edberg
636) NC-17
637) *The Simpsons*
638) a

639) Jim Henson
640) c
641) a
642) d
643) c
644) a
645) b
646) b
647) *Pretty Woman*
648) c
649) c
650) Roald Dahl
651) a 4, b 2, c 1, d 3
652) c
653) b
654) b
655) true
656) true
657) false
658) false
659) false
660) false
661) b
662) c
663) c
664) c
665) d
666) c
667) b
668) d
669) d
670) Duke
671) Nirvana

672) d
673) c
674) Comedy Central
675) c
676) The Congress of People's Deputies of the Soviet Union dissolved
677) c
678) Bill Clinton
679) Magic Johnson
680) b
681) "(Everything I Do) I Do It For You"
682) false—"You Are Not Alone," 1995
683) "Gonna Make You Sweat"
684) a
685) Bonn
686) d
687) b
688) a
689) c
690) Tim Russert
691) c
692) Scott Norwood
693) b
694) Generation X
695) a
696) c
697) a
698) c
699) b
700) b
701) b
702) d
703) Prince Charles
704) b
705) Taylor Lautner
706) d
707) b
708) d

About Applesauce Press

GOOD IDEAS RIPEN WITH TIME. FROM SEED TO HARVEST, APPLESAUCE PRESS CREATES BOOKS WITH BEAUTIFUL DESIGNS, CREATIVE FORMATS, AND KID-FRIENDLY INFORMATION. LIKE OUR PARENT COMPANY, CIDER MILL PRESS BOOK PUBLISHERS, OUR PRESS BEARS FRUIT TWICE A YEAR, PUBLISHING A NEW CROP OF TITLES EACH SPRING AND FALL.

"WHERE GOOD BOOKS ARE READY FOR PRESS"
VISIT US ON THE WEB AT
WWW.CIDERMILLPRESS.COM
OR WRITE TO US AT
12 PORT FARM ROAD
KENNEBUNKPORT, MAINE 04046